Blessings & Peace!

Unemployed

A Memoir

by

Reginald L. Goodwin

Reggie '07

INNERCIRCLE PUBLISHING

Unemployed - A Memoir

ISBN: 0-9762974-5-0

Edition 1

Cover Photos taken by Chad Lilly
Cover Creation by Chad Lilly
Textblock Creation by Stacy Lilly

www.innercirclepublishing.com

Foreword

I've had the disturbing epiphany of reading about blogging and its current impact on our society and world. One fellow got hired because of the software content of his tech geek blog; the other persons got fired because of the creative distain they published about their companies in their blogs. Human Resource departments are making searching the Internet for blog content a common practice in hiring decisions. Blogging is being added into the appendices of companies approved modes of "official communication."

I've been asked often by my wife, "did your blogging cost you the interview/job"? So, I bravely did a Google search on my formal name, Reginald L. Goodwin. Here's some of what "shook out":

www.worldtangsoodo.com/regions/Listing.asp?region=4
www.brown.edu/Students/Tang_Soo_Do/Registry.htm

These are web sites attached to the martial art I teach and study. I'm an Engineering Physics graduate of North Carolina A & T State University, December of 1984 (an Orwellian year, in reflection).

I then did a search on "Reggie Goodwin." I first received mention on some alumni association functions ***http://www.ncatwesternregion.com/chapters.html***. I'm mentioned in several articles on hosting poetry venues (as I do at Mitchie's Fine Art and Frame Gallery every 2nd Saturday from 3 – 5 PM): also innocuous.

This blog began with what you will soon read in the introduction. The conditions that caused my predicament existed, before ***it*** did.

I represent the American worker that feels the "fell clutch of circumstance," to quote Invictus, at or around forty years of age. I bare witness to the fact that despite past performance, college preparation, individual contribution, teamwork, no one is immune to the Leviathan called the global economy and its dictates to save on costs: the largest being employees and benefits. I am an example of the human toll of NAFTA and CAFTA. These are not programs of one party or the other: these are programs that affect the many and enrich the few. If I were to smile and disappear like a "good Cheshire cat" ala "Alice in Wonderland," what has happened to me, what has happened to many, what is and will, in the foreseeable future, *still* happen, will not be corrected

There is no lack of blogs from the unemployed. The experience and the pain is worldwide. The book that follows is my journey, documented on my blog and shared by many that have become outsourced Americans. What I will share with you is a walk of faith that is real, that is true.

Sincerely,
Reginald L. Goodwin
Outsourced American

Table of Contents

Introduction

"Take this kiss upon the brow!
And, in parting from you now,
Thus much let me avow--
You are not wrong who deem
That my days have been a dream;
Yet if hope has flown away
In a night, or in a day,
In a vision, or in none,
Is it therefore the less gone?
All that we see or seem
Is but a dream within a dream."

Edgar Allen Poe, "Dream Within a Dream"

Posted 12/22/2004:

I share an e-mail log I've had with a major technology company:

11/16/2004

Hi-I'd like to schedule a phone screen with you regarding the position that you applied for at (name of company blanked out). At the moment, my schedule is open: Tuesday Nov 16, 2 - 5 Central time, Wednesday Nov 17, 8:30 to 2 and 3 to 5 CST Friday Nov 19, 8 to 5 CST. Please let me know if there is a 30-minute window in there that would work for you, what number I should call, or if you would prefer to contact me. I look forward to hearing from you,

(Name blanked out) Technical Recruiting
(Name of company blanked out)

*****

Reply:

Hello:

How about either 17 November at 10:00 AM or 19 November, same time?

Best regards,
Reggie Goodwin

Home: (number blanked out)
Cell: (number blanked out)

11/17/2004

Reggie-

I'm booked today at that time, so I have you on my calendar for Friday at 10AM. Would you like me to call you at home or on your cell? Also, the resume I have has your last position at (name of previous company blanked out) in 2003. If you have more recent work experience and would like to submit another resume I can replace this version.

thanks-
(Name blanked out)

*****

My reply:

(Name blanked out):

I enjoyed speaking with you on the phone this morning. I hope to progress successfully in the next phone interview with the hiring manager, and eventually (everything going positively) the position at (name of company blanked out).

My work experience has been as a self-employed person. The (name of company blanked out) position I just recently picked up for seasonal work. If you think both are relevant, I will update the resume.

Reggie

11/19/2004

Reggie-

I think the version we have is fine. I forwarded it onto the hiring manager, and I think he is checking around here for people who might have known you at (name of previous company blanked out). Nothing like an inside reference :)

Talk to you soon-
(Name blanked out)

*****

11/22/2004

(Name blanked out),

Any updates?

Reggie

*****

11/23/2004

HR's reply:

You are on the hiring managers list of calls to make - I looked at the tracking sheet this AM.

(name blanked out)

11/30/2004

(Name blanked out):

(Name of hiring manager blanked out) - (forgive me: I believe that is the name of the hiring manager you mentioned in our phone interview) hasn't called me. Has the position been filled?

Regards,
Reggie Goodwin

(Number blanked out) (H): best after 9:00 AM
(Number blanked out) (M): anytime, VM

*****

12/1/2004

HRs reply:

Not yet. We have 2 interviews scheduled for Friday, so my guess is that he is waiting to see what the outcome is of those before spending time wooing anyone else :) I'll try to follow up with you next T or W and let you know what happened.

(Name blanked out)

*****

12/2/2004

(Name blanked out):

I've established (number blanked out) with voice mail through Call Notes (again). Any calls for telephone and/or scheduling of personal interviews can now be left there.

Best regards,
Reggie Goodwin

12/7/2004

(Name blanked out),

I look forward to your reply.

Best regards,
Reggie Goodwin

(Number blanked out) (VM)
(Number blanked out) (Mobile)

*****

HR's reply:

Reggie-

I am sorry to report than an offer was made yesterday, although it has not yet been accepted. We should know 12/17, if you want to email me after that for status.

(Name blanked out)

*****

My reply:

(Name blanked out),

I've been out of work since 26 August 2003 (ironically, the anniversary of my father's death). If you can tell me what defeated my chances to even get a face-to-face interview I'd greatly appreciate it. If not with <name>, the information would be valuable with some other company.

I'd also like to know if it's worth my time (or ------'s) to continue my posting on the job site. Thank you.

Reggie

12/21/2004

The follow-up referred to my calling the HR rep directly on 12/17/2004:

Reggie-

I promised that I would follow up with you as soon as I knew something. We made an offer yesterday to a candidate that we interviewed back in early November, and he accepted. The position is considered filled and will be officially closed once I get his paperwork back.

I'm sorry - I know you are disappointed. I hope you will continue to watch the (name of company blanked out) job board and apply for other positions you are qualified for.

Best Regards-
(Name blanked out)

*****

My reply:

(Name blanked out),

I'm a little confused in your interview procedure: why was I phone interviewed if you already had (now I'm counting) three candidates with the 2 the previous Friday and now the November candidate?

Forgive me. This answer doesn't change my current employment prospects. I need something with a little more substance.

Sunday, December 26, 2004 will be 1 year and four months to the date I've been unemployed; underemployed working odd jobs I'm severely overqualified for (like UPS).

Reggie

As of 12/27/2004, no reply from the HR Technical Recruiter (I think she's on Christmas vacation)…

Many would say I've "burned my bridges." They'd say I should have held my tongue and applied for as many jobs on the web site as possible.

Some points to make here:

1. I posted to this site about a month after my lay off, redoing and polishing my resume at Drake, Beam, Morin and Associates (they'd advise me to hold my peace as well).

2. Up until the phone call - generated by her - I'd receive e-mails about job matches that I apparently qualified for. I'd answer yes, of course, and then would hear nothing back or that the job has been filled and the rec closed. OK.

3. This is the first REAL person I've talked to in over a year on this site. This company could have made it easier for me to stay in Austin, Texas. I'm trying to maintain stability for my youngest son to finish high school (currently in the seventh grade). I've gotten offers to leave and if I didn't own a local business or have a family, I would have been GONE a long time ago.

4. She stated, "You are on the hiring managers list of calls to make - I looked at the tracking sheet this AM" on November 23.

5. I recall in a phone conversation, the hiring manager was walking my resume around to "see if anyone knew me at my former company." Since it had about 13,000 workers at one time of my employment, there was a fair chance the manager wasn't successful. If anything derogatory (can't think of anything) was said, I believe I have LEGAL rights against slander.

Trust me. I'm trying to stay positive.

I'm working in shipping in a warehouse larger than 10 football fields; on a production floor of conveyer belts, full of cursing workers, and a delicate ballet between the forces of static and kinetic friction I can only refer to as "a controlled avalanche!"

The physicality is the only thing I appreciate. It allows me to beat the *snot* out of cardboard boxes, sling them through space, yell a little myself and vent any frustrations about my circumstances at inanimate, unfeeling objects.

Trust me. I'm trying to stay positive. But when you're making 1/5 of what you made as a professional engineer per hour, when you're up at 3 AM when the rest of the world is sleeping, when you've seen your retirement and investments dwindle to dust, that can make you a little testy. I probably need a time out!

Chapter 1
Great Games of Cat and Mouse

"This is the way the world ends
This is the way the world ends
This is the way the world ends
Not with a bang but a whimper."

T.S. Eliot, "The Hollow Men"

In the syndicated cartoon strip, Dilbert (R) (www.dilbert.com), Dilbert's cat, ubiquitously named *Catbert* is the "Evil HR director." One of Catbert's favorite games was playing with employees - as a cat, the employees likened unto mice - before informing them of their severance from the unnamed corporation where Dilbert and his coworkers were employed.

The funny thing about corporations is their preoccupation with making money. I say funny because the last thing anyone in the upper echelons would think of cutting are spiffs, bonuses and "accelerators" (never understood this compensation) that management, from directors to the CEO get regardless of the companies or stock's performance. This is usually the same management that made the decisions, greased the palms and caused us all to execute the company vision on these same decisions that now had us in a deficit (oops).

The Senior Vice Presidents, Vice Presidents and Directors like us received performance reviews, which I can only assume were glowing. The CEO's review was presumably from the stockholders of the corporation. His performance was rated on the performance of the company. Depending on his/her employment contract, firing him/her could be easy or costly. That's easy if you happen to be part of a debacle like Enron (a no-brainer there).

Also costly, in light of the recent report of Fannie Mae's former CEO Franklin Raines and their former CFO J. Timothy Howard. Raines will receive $1.4 million dollars per year for life (he's a spry 55) and the former CFO Howard will only get $432,852 per year. Howard is 56. See ***http://www.usatoday.com/money/companies/management/2004-12-28-fannie-usat_x.htm***.

The underlings (I was one of them) would get a performance review that was supposedly, a reflection of our job performance. Then we were ranked alongside persons of the same engineering grade. In a quarterly review, I was told everything was going fine and that my score was well above the midrange.

Around the end of the first quarter and the beginning of the second quarter of 2003, we lost our Vice President, if you want to call it losing him. We were informed he was finding "other opportunities within the company." Loose translation: find a job before we sever you! I hope he was successful.

Our new director was German. For fun and not to his face, we called him "Colonel Clink" (from Hogan's Heroes, I'm dating myself). He had a forewarned reputation as a "hatchet man." I never witnessed a smile on his face. He was always very serious, very grim. Hence, if you're a student of history, my reference to the Great Game in the title.

Our great game of cat and mouse began with so-called *Communications Meetings*. I recall knowing LESS after the communications meeting than I knew before walking in. One brilliant engineer decided to break the silence with a carefully coded question for the Colonel:

"Do you think the organization is of an efficient size to be managed effectively?"

The Colonel's reply:

"Every change in an organization takes some... pain to accomplish the greater good!"

I thought: *List this man for the 2003 Darwin Award for the DUMBEST question a human being could say during an economic downturn!*

And the great game would continue with our *communications meetings*, an oxymoron. After one and a half hours of Power Point charts and heavy German accents, your eyes glazed over. If any important information was communicated, you usually compared notes in the cafeteria later. What you didn't get, your fellow worker probably caught.

Since were weren't getting anything from the meetings, we circulated our own rumors: "I heard they're going to get us in the auditorium and lay us all off from there! Our division is getting dissolved." Most of us had street contacts with former employees of the Colonel or current secretaries that couldn't keep their mouths shut around the lunch table. If you've ever played the game in elementary school of giving the first person a note and having them whisper it to the next person, then checking the accuracy of the information with the last person in the whisper line, you can understand the distortions when intentions were not communicated clearly. Any bolder questions regarding downsizing, lay offs or division dissolving was parried with the "necessary pain for the greater good" proverb analogy.

It was during this time I wrote in my analog journal (which I've kept since college). I composed some thoughts about the stress I was going through at not knowing what the future held for my family and me. I'll share those thoughts with you now:

<u>Code Orange</u>

I stare
At another "Tableau Rasa"
Purchased at Barnes and Noble
For \$4.95 (plus tax)
Taking respite once
Again on a porcelain
God listening
To the accounts
Of the original
Tejas inhabitants:
One of the fellow's
Wife is due soon.

Yet
The rest I swoon
From is not the result of a
Blown-up pager:

It is the stranger
Silence... that
Allows you to hear
The rumors about your
Performance and intercept
All stares as broken
Conversations about you...

The elation
Of a job well done
Flits by
In nanoseconds
That “flip-flop”
Registers on
Computer chip
Architecture
Couldn’t keep pace with.

You’ve just spent time:
Talking to a young mother
And her two-year-old boy
(She has another) and
Looks like she’s too young
To have the one
Slaughtering his pizza
As he smiles
At you in Schlotsky’s...
Gave her my wife’s number
Since she and her hubby are
Looking for a home
In Wimberley
(Wife’s a real estate agent);

Finding the last
Anthology of the
Austin International Poetry Festival
Barnes and Noble had
Of Di-Verse-City

Where you FINALLY
Appear on page 100
(Perks of being a board member -
Bought it for my mother for
Mother's Day)...

Assaulted by WORDS
Of Whitman, Hughes, Saul Williams, Beau Sea, Regie Gilson
As decisions become as clouded as the
Overcast skies viewed.

Enraptured by a fellow
Artist - Adrienne - young
Enough to be your daughter,
Yet by her neo 70s dress
And quiet demeanor
Stressed you to ask:
"Are you a poet?"
(Yes, and an artist, too!)
Her surreal exhibit sounds
Intriguing and will go
Up soon. She quips its
The "please help Adrienne
With her bills exhibit."
I promise to stop by
Again and look.)

Mailing the anthology
With one of several
Mother's Day cards
Purchased at
Barnes and Noble,
Sending it priority
Mail and walking
Out proud: I usually
Have to do Federal Express!

Driving back, I catch

A fat, almost tooth-less
Cat with a sign saying:

"This just in: homeless
Consumers invade Iraq."

It makes me laugh, but not as the MBA in my old piece:

The Other Foot

Because I don't have to descend to his level:
His is the terror of day-to-day,
Staying alive,
While mine is Al Jolson
On a downsizing Silicon stage
Beveled at the corners to make
The transition look smooth,
While grandsons of founders
Make spiffs and accelerators
Incalculable over
The corpses of an
"Asset lite" rage...

The only difference is the space between us and the 4-runner steed beneath me:

He is my left foot,
I am his right.

Chapter 2
Denouement

From www.m-w.com:
Denouement - Function: noun
Etymology: French dénouement, literally, untying, from Middle French desnouement, from desnouer to untie, from Old French desnoer, from des- de- + noer to tie, from Latin nodare, from nodus knot -- more at NODE

1: the final outcome of the main dramatic complication in a literary work

2: the outcome of a complex sequence of events

I named this chapter denouement. A testament to my tenth grade English teacher, Velma Williamson, I recall her simplified version of the above definition as "a falling action"; "the story climax." You get the whole point of the tale after hanging on breathlessly page after page. Some authors, even more dramatically, describe it and the conclusion of a story as "a little death": an appropriate metaphor.

The Colonel continued with his non-communications meetings, glazed eyes and all from March through August of 2003. We missed one meeting in June due to his having to go to a meeting at our corporate headquarters. He - that is, his secretary - sent an apologetic e-mail stating he was sorry we'd have to miss the June meeting. Hallelujah.

By July, we all got bulk e-mail from corporate communications. There would be a reorganization of the business units and an involuntary severance before the end of the third quarter. Since July is the beginning of most companies third quarters, you can't plan vacations to conveniently fall on the fated day. Our street contacts were mum. Now, the secrecy of the corporate animus rivaled that of the White House or the Central Intelligence Agency. The attitude from most workers was heavy with despair. That became the central theme of conversations around lunch, either on or off campus. Actually, off campus lunches, though more expensive became more frequent to say things outside of the company that were not quite "PC."

"How are they making this decision?"

"My last review... I mean, I think I scored OK and all."

"You know what p----s me off? I notice they never lay *themselves* off, and many times it was their dumb decisions that caused the problems!"

"On top of that, they get bonuses. Do you know how long it's been since I've seen a bonus? Centuries. And I haven't lived THAT long!"

They. Them.

I watched a friend become one. He'd started out as a decent engineer. Then the dreaded thing happened: he was promoted to Section Manager.

After a succession of promotions and accolades, he became an Operations Manager of one of our factories. During process yield meetings, I'd watch him grill engineer after engineer, pestering them and hammering them until he could catch them in a technical faux pas, an "aha" moment that he'd ride until the engineer felt about two inches tall leaving the podium. It makes my skin crawl recalling some of his comments:

"What the HELL did you think you were doing?"

"Am I paying you for incompetence, or results?"

"Sit down. Those results are absolute bull----! Come back when you have something of merit to report. Come to my office after this meeting!"

"You were abusing your lab time!" The hapless engineer explained he wasn't and used the time to solve a yield problem that BENEFITED the company. "Did anyone else get in the lab while you were overusing your time? Well, then I still say you abused your lab time!"

Needless to say, my former friend/monster had a lot of professional turnover.

"...Reorganization of the business units and an involuntary severance before the end of the third quarter."

August...

All of my engineering projects dried up like a sunflower wilting in the Texas summer heat. I logged as much time as I could on the test floor. I attended meetings and tried to insert myself into new projects, new platforms.

I was so distraught, I went to our business unit's HR manager. She was a petite woman, swarthy and lovely, obviously of Hispanic ancestry despite her married Christian name. I made an appointment to talk with her. I wanted answers and I asked her for them. "Am I on this list?" "Why didn't you give us a choice of voluntary severance?" "Don't you realize you're playing with peoples lives and incomes here?" Her face - I'd seen it before - on my cat: an armor-piercing stare of determination. I'd usually see it on my cat before... she'd kill a mouse.

"I know how you must feel. I'm afraid I can't answer that." She said it with a staccato reminiscent of a dutiful Stepford/Android wife.

Before the end, as with my father's death four years prior (the anniversary of his demise coming soon on the twenty-sixth of the month of August) humans I feel, have premonitions of the end of things. This verse chronicled my feelings at that time:

Horizon R.O.A.D

(Retired On Active Duty)

On the road going to nowhere
There is static on every channel,
No frantic gestures from road-raged drivers spouting nonsense.

The only relent and belief
Is that you are the only driver
Gazing at a horizon without event or relief.

On the road going to nowhere
Dark, gray cliffs line the side
Of empty streets;
No accidents to avoid,
No pedestrians (to miss) or meet.
A world void of color, inhabited by no one other than you...

On the road going to nowhere
Is the stark-raving terror of reflection:
Remembering life's other goals and directions
Requiring risk and FAITH.
Somewhere, you lost your courage and did what was SAFE.

As you sweat in SUV expectations
Not reaching for Porches or Vet,

Will you stay on this road out of fear and despair?
Desperately clinging to the gray color-void
Surety
Of
The road going to nowhere?

Chapter 3
A Falling Action

"Yet ah! Why should they know their fate?
Since sorrow never comes too late,
And happiness too swiftly flies.
Thought would destroy their paradise.
No more; where ignorance is bliss,
'Tis folly to be wise."

Thomas Gray, "Ode on a Distant Prospect of Eton College"

The last communications meeting was Thursday, August 19, 2003. We were shown the new structure of the business unit. The re-org had finally been accomplished.

Everyone's names were on the new charts!

Granted, my Operations Manager was demoted in grade to a group level manager. My group level manager was moved to program management. What was immediately infuriating to everyone concerned is that for all the drama, we were still in the same positions, still in the same job functions.

Or, so we thought.

August 26, 2003. This was the fourth year anniversary of my father's death. I remember the trips I took between Texas and North Carolina to see him as cancer ate at his cells. I saw a man I once looked to for strength and wisdom slowly wither away. I saw once hard muscles atrophy and become languid. The steady frame that taught me how to box I now lowered gingerly into a tub to bathe as he once did me. I saw the strong will that kept me from experimenting with the drugs that ravaged my community become weak and frightened. I saw a gray mane fall to the pillows revealing a head made bald, not by choice. I saw death and could do nothing, NOTHING to stop its natural process.

I called him "Pop" ala Elroy Jetson from the sixties cartoon show. He was a smoker and had been so since the age of ten years old. He stopped at 65.

I called him Pop as a mantra, a breath prayer to counteract the years of tobacco and alcohol abuse. I called him Pop because I calculated his age from my birth: 37 until his demise at 74 on August 26, 1999. I just turned 37 when I received the call from my mother: "he's gone!" I was literally half his age.

I'd been in contact with emotions I'd denied for so long - a tumultuous, agonizing pang of tears that would not stop. I would try to anesthetize the pain with teaching martial arts, poetry, sex, wine - no drug that offered a temporary fix seemed appropriate. That night, 11:27 PM central time, I collapsed into the arms of my wife and children. Pop, grandpa was gone.

So today was the anniversary of his death. I was four years removed from the event and was curious as to how I would commemorate his passing. At each visit to his grave in North Carolina, I'd become a hopeless mess! Apologizing for not being strong enough, agonizing over every sin I'd ever committed, feeling that I hadn't measured up to his expectations.

Today I was in Texas, 1,500 miles from his gravesite. I was in control of my emotions; melancholy...

"Reggie, could you come with me please?"

My former manager had a somber look on his face. I knew what was transpiring.

My former Operations Manager had tried valiantly to find me another position within the company. The severance did not come as a surprise; just the day they chose:

August 26, 2003

My former manager led me to my former operations manager to a walled office with someone from HR. The door was respectfully closed. Both men were visibly upset - almost to tears - as the HR rep (not the Catbert/Stepford wife Android woman, but a male underling) reviewed all the paperwork now assigned to me discreetly behind that closed door.

Not to be insensitive: It was the closest thing in recent memory for me, as a man likened to the crime of rape.

Ironically, I'd read an article in Fortune Magazine, ominously titled "Finished at Forty" ***http://www.fortune.com/fortune/articles***

/0,15114,375941,00.html. They were surprised at how quickly my office affects fit neatly into one box.

If you study the art of war diligently (for me, over two decades), a sense of your surroundings develops. I'd moved out slowly, prepared for what seemed inevitable.

On that day, August 26, 2003, I'd just turned 41 twelve days before.

The day after my forty-first birthday, I wrote this poem. As I stated in the previous chapter and somewhat above, I think humans have a built-in sixth sense of dreaded things on the horizon. I am sharing with you, the reader, what I was feeling at the time. Downturns in the economy can make you a little prophetic and a lot crazy! As the last line suggests, I'd received my... falling action.

Laughing Through Wormholes

I wanted one door to close and another to open.

I wanted
To plunge through its orifice having intercourse
In lands flowing with milk and honey.

I wanted
To steer my own rudder, working cow utters
Wearing protective suits and screens
Occasionally getting stung by honeybees.

I wanted
To stop acting like an engineer
Intellectually propping up numb skull
Regimes by numb and dumber
"Pointy-haired" managers (see: www.dilbert.com)
Straight from Hades
Torments and screams...

I wanted
The death-rattle games to end,

Played by "Catbert - evil HR directors"
To my chagrin...

I wanted
To flee the tomb of innuendoes; rumors and gossip,

I wanted
To stop hearing the doubts
Seeded in my mind by doublethink demons
Using my talent for their fat wallet profit.

I wanted
Good health and financial independence,
Dependent on my God-given gifts and not
"Leave it to Beaver"
"Ozzie and Harriet"
To-make-THEM-comfortable-with-my-kind
Riffs.

I wanted
To fill my days with the hot haze
Of door-to-door graze, knocking, clocking
Fulfilling my dreams.

I wanted
Time to think and self-publish
The great American novel, essay, anthology, chapbook...

I wanted
Time to design one B-A-D web page
To which others would link and look.

I wanted
To see my dreams and my life fulfilled,
My children and my wife have FAITH in me.

I wanted
Off the long, unending road going to nowhere,
Off the steep roller coaster to obsidian oblivion...

I wanted to STOP it!

Chapter 4
The Working Poor

"Economy Not Kind to the Working Poor"
By Anna Varela

<u>The Atlanta Journal-Constitution</u>
(http://www.truthout.org/docs_04/123104J.shtml)

The aspect of a lay off: you don't think of the next step to do with your money, though you are counseled to do just that.

You don't think about the fact that your benefits for doctors' visits will run out with the time they've attached to your severance.

Melancholy is numbness. It's neither maniacally panicked nor remotely calm.

Even if and when you are counseled wisely about your money, the most obvious thing to do is to downsize your lifestyle. Thoreau said, "simplify, simplify, simplify."

What works for writing assignments doesn't always work for living in suburban neighborhoods after living most of your life in a... hood.

It's a pride issue. I'd worked hard, sacrificed much time to the pursuit of a degree in Engineering Physics. I can't TELL you how many parties I avoided for what I now reflect on as above average grades.

I had a window in my room that faced east towards the sunrise. It subtly told me that a new day always dawned despite my circumstances.

I recall every safe house and drug/candy store a character by the name of "Po' Charlie" had in my neighborhood (or, "hood").

I vividly remember the announcement of police raids at Charlie's safe houses; how they would find nothing. I remember cheering for Charlie, not the police.

He was Robin Hood, though I never benefited from his largesse. He was merely strong enough to go up against "the pigs" -- a metaphor from the 60s and the Panthers.

As I look back on him, he was a leech sucking the vital blood out of a community. He was a vulture feasting on the dead bodies of the addicted. But, I digress.

You realize you are the working poor when you apply for... food stamps. Now, the stamp is a debit card with a balance you must not exceed each month. In downsizing the types of foods you'd usually get, the choices left aren't very nutritious.

The upside -- it forces you to budget, which in this long personal night I'm walking through is probably the only good thing about it.

Chapter 5
The Return of Catbert

"If the radiance of a thousand suns
were to burst at once into the sky
that would be like the splendor of the Mighty one --
I am become Death,
The shatterer of Worlds."

J. Robert Oppenheimer (from the Bhagavad-Gita)
July 16, 1945 when the first atomic bomb was tested

I think I just lost it.

I'm sure of it now. I had her number and I called it.

If you remember in my intro, I corresponded with an HR rep. The initial e-mails were very positive and I thought... I thought her company'd hire me.

I smelled a rat! You see, my resume is two pages on and it says the ubiquitous phrase in it "Senior Engineer."

I paraphrase the following conversation from memory:

*****

HR: Hello?

Me: Hello, am I speaking to ____________?

HR: Well, hello. How are you doing?

Me: I'm inquiring about something.

HR: And, what might that be?

Me: Why I was passed over for the position.

HR: I'm not at liberty to discuss...

Me: LOOK, lady! I've been out of work for over a year. I have NO health benefits. I've exhausted my retirement just to pay bills. You don't live my life!

HR: Sir, SIR! Calm down.

Me: I'm as CALM as the circumstances allow me to be.

HR: We... we're in the same boat.

Me: How do you figure that? You're in an air-conditioned building in a cubicle with a computer...

HR: I'm a contract worker, sir. Once the company hires all their needs, I'll be laid off.

Me: I'm all tears.

HR: Sir... you're not serving yourself. As a matter-of-fact: if you persist in this course, I can put in a recommendation to not hire you!

Me: "Catbert" was obviously spawned from YOUR personality.

HR: SIR! I can... appreciate your dilemma. This is a rough economy. But, if I were to put in this recommendation, it will travel. You wouldn't be able to get hired by any firm in the city; possible the state... possibly further.

Me: You really enjoy your work, don't you?

HR: I'm just telling you to calm down. I won't put in the recommendation unless you continue to insist on this line of conversation. The company doesn't want to hire unstable people.

Me: ..... Goodbye.

*****

That was it.

My rant stopped cold by the cold logic of Catbert's power. *I can ruin your life.* I could feel her predatory stare through the phone. I hung up, not because I didn't have more to say, but what else could I say?

What happened to engineering? When did it become a thespian performance art? Even in unemployment I must put on the positive

Step-n-Fetch smile, grinning from ear-to-ear, dance my jig and mouth YASSA, MASSA. My jaws were tight, just like they were when I had my so-called job...

When my wife lost her job, it was kind of sweet. We pulled in our budget and saved where we could. She was home going on field trips to pick berries with the women in the cul-de-sac. My youngest son loved the fact that his mom was at home and he didn't have to go to daycare, one of the pulled-in expenses.

The point is she had emotional support.

I recall "The Manpower Series" by TD Jakes. In it, he made a black-and-white declaration about men and women: men being in most general cases positional and women being *relational.*

Women: "How many children do you have?"
Men: "What do you DO for a living?"

Do... what defines you now, months after a lay off? It used to be the morning commute, the coffee at Starbucks, the banter before the 8:30 AM engineering meeting. It used to be lunch with your coworkers and conversations. It used to be the projects you were assigned and the sense of accomplishment at their completion.

Do... some of us I've heard invested money in either T2 or T1 connections, bought software they used at work as a means to "consult." They end up instead checking their e-mails for the job leads they've sent out on a souped-up computer. But, consulting gigs are going overseas as well. I've heard of depression and at least one suicide (I hope it was a rumor, an urban myth).

I... went a little crazy. But I am convinced, Catbert DOES NOT in any way identify with what I'm going through right now.

Chapter 6
Reds

"And God said: Go down, Death, go down,
Go down to Savannah, Georgia,
Down in Yamacraw,
And find Sister Caroline.
She's borne the burden and heat of the day,
She's labored long in my vineyard,
And she's tired--
She's weary--
Go down, Death, and bring her to me."

James Weldon Johnson, "Go Down, Death"

This is something I have to get off my chest.

Maybe it will help someone. I'm hoping it will help me.

Reds is a shooting range in Pflugerville, Texas. I somehow find myself passing it often now that I'm "free."

I've been on the range before. I usually shot a Gloc 9 millimeter.

I see myself in this vision: I go in the door from the parking lot. I purchase time on the range and ammo. I see myself talking to the proprietors of the range. We joke briefly.

I get my ear protection; adjust my glasses and head on the range.

I mount my target and send it via the automatic pulley down range.

I load my weapon, careful to point the muzzle at all times down range.

I release the safety, lifting the weapon, aligning the front and rear sights. I practice "BRASS": breath, relax, aim, slack (the trigger finger), squeeze (the trigger finger). Repeat.

I pull the target back up range. I inspect it to adjust my aim and possibly my sights from the shot group.

I send my target via the automatic pulley down range.

I load my weapon, careful to point the muzzle at all times down range.

I release the safety, lifting the weapon, aligning the front and rear sights. I practice "BRASS": breath, relax, aim, slack (the trigger finger), squeeze (the trigger finger).

My universe is crimson - the gray of the range is replaced by a space of blood. My head erupts into molten lava as the smell of sulfur invades my olfactory. I fall.

I practiced "BRASS": breath, relax, aim, slack (the trigger finger), squeeze (the trigger finger). No one suspected until they have to call EMS… too late.

I always awake from the vision with a bolt of consciousness. Lately, the visions have been during the day... as I drive past the range.

I wish I could say this was an "April Fools" joke. I hope it helps someone. I hope it helps me.

Chapter 7
Heathcliff Huxtable

"A word to the wise ain't necessary –
it's the stupid ones that need the advice."

Bill Cosby

I am looking at the images of the houseless (as I stand corrected by a shade tree mechanic: he is not "homeless" as he pointed to the wooded area where he comfortably lays his head with his fellows at night). These are not images I see only on television: I see them alarmingly closer to my suburban home, alarmingly resembling my neighbors.

"Nick at Nite" has run through all ten years of the Cosby Show and is now on the initial reruns dating from 1984 when Rudy was cute. Now, Keisha Knight-Pullam is starring with Queen Latifah in "Beauty Shop" and had a magazine expose in what looked like skimpy bikini fashion (saw it at the grocery store: didn't buy it).

Nineteen eighty-four was not only the year I graduated with my Physics degree, we were treated to positive images of black family life by Bill Cosby and Phylicia Rashad.

As I understand it, getting Cliff cast as a doctor and Claire as a lawyer took a heated confrontation by "The Cos" with the show's producers. They wanted another "ghetto sitcom" similar to *Good Times* (which, John Amos left the show because his TV family never left the ghetto); *The Jefferson's*, George never left his ignorant acting ways from when he was neighbors to Archie Bunker though he'd made it to the "deluxe apartment in the sky," and lastly *Sanford and Son*, with Fred faking heart attacks to Elizabeth and Lamont tripping through life clueless (I hear he is or at one time was a preacher).

I was twenty-three, young, impressionable and scared to death. I was going in the US Air Force as a Communications Officer - a specialty everyone says was a good choice. The problem is, I didn't choose it. I digress.

Cliff and Claire became the black Ozzie and Harriett. We were glued to a tube that stated simply "you can have a successful black sitcom without the general stereotypes." Unfortunately, we substituted new ones.

What I mean is Cliff and Claire represented the "new" rich in black America. Most of us were just beginning the steps taking us towards the middle class. With the exception of the occasional "glitch" with each of their TV children, they resolved most problems in thirty minutes or less in time for the final scene.

I now realize the Huxtable clan were both a good thing... and bad.

Good in that I could view The Cos in his element: comedy. I could laugh and take my mind off my troubles for just a moment.

Here's the bad [all opinions mine]:

The Cosby Show became the litmus test for the so-called "color-blind society" that conservatives, black and white, began touting in the eighties. Unfortunately, the success of the show was warped into the foundation for attacks on affirmative action and set aside programs for black business owners to get a leg up (like major corporations *still* do with tax abatements).

Bad in that Heathcliff and Claire Huxtable became an ideal I subconsciously reached for and would do anything to fulfill. That image became an idol.

Bad in that we went from one extreme of "ghetto fabulous" to "suburban somnambulism." We went from no hope of getting out of our dire straits to obviously never having been there. We went from being held down by "the man" to "lifting ourselves by our own bootstraps." I know Dr. Cosby never meant to have that effect on the black community, but I suspect overreach is part of the Urban League's report that our net worth is 1/10 that of whites still... in the Twenty-first century: trying to be like the Huxtables.

So, I find myself juxtaposed between the reality and the fantasy of the Huxtable image. I am unemployed. I am trying to get a business off the ground that like many of us began as a hobby, an outlet after work. I am looking at the real possibility of loosing the business and the house unless some drastic, RADICAL changes take place. I know what one of those changes is: selling my 4-runner. My wife makes a good point: what are we going to do when you NEED a car? My simple answer is "get one." With what resources at my disposal at the time, God and truly God, only knows. I know the other change is to lease or sell our home. Even with her working and it being refinanced out the wazzo, we can't afford the mortgage.

I feel like the father with the son possessed by a demon, crying out: "Lord, I believe, help thou my unbelief!"

I don't know how God will get me my wealth. I do know it's needed now!

Chapter 8
Mr. Mom

"Had I the heavens' embroidered cloths,
Enwrought with golden and silver light,
The blue and the dim and the dark cloths
Of night and light and the half-light,
I would spread the cloths under your feet:
But I, being poor, have only my dreams;
I have spread my dreams under your feet;
Tread softly because you tread on my dreams."

William Butler Yeats, "The Wind Among the Reeds: He wishes for the Cloths of Heaven"

I've been unemployed now for 1 year, 11 months and 4 days as of 30 July 2005 (today).

I'm really getting tired of hr reps, headhunters, recruiters calling about "I saw your resume on Job.com, Monster.com, Careerbuilder.com, dbm.com", etc., etc., ad nauseum.

You have this... hope that springs up when a headhunter calls. It's after all in his or her best interest to place you in said position for their commission checks.

First, it was Target regarding a logistics position. "I don't have experience in that area," I said. "I know, we're going to try to sell your soft skills as a people person..."

So, I go through the phone screen with Target. I've looked at the web site. I've researched the company and its commitment to diversity; its impact on the communities it operates in.

Then, the recruiter gives me the bad news: "They said there wasn't a good fit between your skill sets and what they were looking for." Isn't that what I JUST said about two paragraphs ago?

This chapter is titled "Mr. Mom" because of an apparent role reversal.

I'm not the only black male in this boat. Two friends are finding themselves the caregivers and their mates the breadwinners.

I've always prepared breakfast and dinners. It was fine when I had a job and my masculinity was intact.

False hope extended is worse than no hope at all. It's a striptease: a hard-on after the performance with nowhere to go.

Now, it's a black firm from Georgia. I researched their site. They're listed with Black Enterprise Magazine. The recruiter sounds like a brother! The position is with Home Depot in their store leadership program. Starting is $80 - 85K, plus benefits. That's more than I made as an engineer.

Reality: My business is within a week of closing, despite the prayers I've solicited from the Internet, the prayer team (experts in this area), the three days of fasting (OK, I was desperate) and the amounts of 401 (k), severance, 60 plus hours a week I've devoted to making myself successful.

Reality: It looks like I'm going to have to be Mr. Mom as my wife kills herself selling for Plantation Homes (not kidding). She thinks she can do it, and I'm sure she can.

The causality in all of this is my male ego. I have a need to succeed and provide for my family. It's an in-bred instinct: the weaker males faced extinction in the clan, did not mate with the most attractive and in some extreme cases were EATEN by their kinsmen!

An open comment to hr reps, headhunters, recruiters and Catbert Evil HR Directors: this is what you're dealing with when you call a guy that's been out of the game for two years, is developing dish panned hands and a disturbing tolerance for the SOAP Network!

So now, with the hope, I wait. I waited Friday until I could not stand it and called the firm with kids (running a summer camp) screaming in my ear. The do-wop song "Rescue Me" comes to mind. My revised resume has been forwarded to the rep over the Home Depot account to make a determination about doing a phone screen.

Ah, the infamous phone screen. And so, I wait...

Chapter 9
On Becoming

"Holding anger is a poison. It eats you from inside. We think that hating is a weapon that attacks the person who harmed us. But hatred is a curved blade. And the harms we do, we do to ourselves."

Mitch Alborn, "The Five People You Meet in Heaven"

Suffice to say, I was not offered the phone screen for the Home Depot position.

However, it has made me consider hiring a lawyer.

I received a call from a headhunting firm. [They] got my resume from careerbuilder.com. They asked me for an updated version of my resume. I obliged the rep. I was confident I could sail through the interview and out of my financial morass.

"I'm sorry, sir. We rejected your resume on the basis of... you are overqualified."

I say, "I've been out of work for two years. YOU called ME. What is your definition of over qualification?"

"You're overqualified, sir, because of your years of experience."

"Just what does that mean?"

"Well, the position requires 6 - 10 years of total work experience... you have more."

"So, are you saying I'm overqualified, or that I'm too old?" I've been working since I was sixteen years old. That's either 22, or 26 years. If they tabulate from my age at graduation, that's 28 - 32 years.

"You're overqualified, sir, because of your years of experience."

"I see. Thank you."

I called information and contacted a lawyer. The math just doesn't add up and two years of blogging is patience enough for anyone.

Chapter 10
"It Has To Be Blatant"

"The mass of men lead lives of quiet desperation.
What is called resignation is confirmed desperation.
From the desperate city you go into the desperate country
and have to console yourself with the bravery
of minks and muskrats.
A stereotyped but unconscious despair is concealed
even under what are called the games and
amusements of mankind.
There is no play in them, for this comes after work.
But it is a characteristic of wisdom not to do desperate things."

Henry David Thoreau, "Walden, Chapter 1, Economy"

"Facts About Age Discrimination"
http://www.eeoc.gov/facts/age.html

The Age Discrimination in Employment Act of 1967 (ADEA) protects individuals who are 40 years of age or older from employment discrimination based on age. The ADEA's protections apply to both employees and job applicants. Under the ADEA, it is unlawful to discriminate against a person because of his/her age with respect to any term, condition, or privilege of employment -- including, but not limited to, hiring, firing, promotion, layoff, compensation, benefits, job assignments, and training.

"It is also unlawful to retaliate against an individual for opposing employment practices that discriminate based on age or for filing an age discrimination charge, testifying, or participating in any way in an investigation, proceeding, or litigation under the ADEA.

"The ADEA applies to employers with 20 or more employees, including state and local governments. It also applies to employment agencies and to labor organizations, as well as to the federal government."

However, Mr. Bobby R. Taylor (***www.taylor-law.com***) says, "It has to be blatant." From this quote describing age discrimination from the EEOC, I don't read that.

You read it for yourself. I've posted the memo below for your review. Mr. Taylor, as black and as bald as I am spent 20 minutes with a white couple before me dressed casually in jeans and canvas pants. He might have spent 20 seconds with me dressed in a business suit. "Just cut to the chase and I'll see if I can help you." I paraphrased the memo below. He "didn't have enough to go on. They may have a reason: they may not want to pay for older employees and are looking for college fresh outs." But, that's not age discrimination. Amazing clairvoyance from Mr. Taylor's "cutting to the chase," considering the lawyer never bothered to read my memo:

Memo for Record, 8 August 2005
Re: Corporate Plus Executive Search Firm/Age Discrimination

To Whom It May Concern:

A Mr. Levan Johnson of Corporate Plus Executive Search Firm contacted me Monday, 25 July 2005. My initial contact was apparently via e-mail at 10:25 AM CST (see E-mail). That was followed up with a call on my cell phone at approximately 11:10 AM.

Mr. Johnson informed me of a Leadership Training Program with a Fortune 15 corporation that his company represented (again, see E-mail). I was chosen for my resume on CareerBuilder.com and it's mentioning of my four years of prior management experience in the United States Air Force where I managed 85 persons in a four-year period.

Mr. Johnson understandably wanted an updated copy of my resume: "What have you been doing since 2003?" I'd been laid off from my job. I admitted I'd been running a business – he called me right in the middle of administrating a martial arts summer camp at the park. He said that experience would also be attractive since the Leadership Training Program was a store management position with their client, Home Depot.

I revised my resume and sent it the same day for Mr. Johnson (see 2nd E-mail). I've also included the revised resume.

Not hearing anything, I called Mr. Johnson that Friday, 29 July 2005 to follow-up on the status of my resume. He forwarded me to a Walter, who was over the division responsible for the Home Depot account.

Walter informed me that the resume had been forwarded and I should hear something soon regarding the next step – a telephone screen. I was informed if I did not hear anything that Friday, I'd definitely hear something conclusive on Monday.

“You’re overqualified based on your years of experience,” was the call and the statement from Mr. Johnson. I asked for clarification, as I could see I am probably overqualified with an Engineering Physics bachelors and 10-plus years experience as an engineer in the semiconductor industry. “No, sir. You’re overqualified based on your years of experience. The position is looking for someone with a total work experience of 6 – 10 years. You have more.”

I did the math in my head. I’ve worked since the age of 16 and I graduated college at 22: that’s either a person age 22 – 26 years or age 28 – 32 years. I will be forty-three Sunday, 14 August 2005. “Is that another way of saying ‘I’m old”?

“No, sir. You’re overqualified based on your years of experience,” he repeated hesitantly. “That’s the total work experience our client is looking for. We will keep your resume on file for other opportunities that are a better fit for your background.”

I said, “Thank you.” I hung up and called information for the number to the Law offices of Bobby R. Taylor, Attorney. END

Mr. Taylor extended his hand as I walked out of his office. I did not reciprocate, interrupted by a call on my mobile phone. He informed his secretary I did not need to pay the $50 consult fee. A rather small, gracious gesture.

I must thank Mr. Taylor for his commentary. You can’t pay for this brand of cosmic comedy anywhere!

Chapter 11
My Day

"…let the day perish wherein I was born…"

Job 3: 2

Job 3: 1 – 7: After this opened Job his mouth, and cursed his day.

And Job spoke, and said, let the day perish wherein I was born, and the night [in which] it was said, there is a man-child conceived.

Let that day be darkness, let not God regard it from above, neither let the light shine upon it.

Let darkness and the shadow of death stain it; let a cloud dwell upon it; let the blackness of the day terrify it.

As [for] that night, let darkness seize upon it; let it not be joined unto the days of the year, let it not come into the number of the months.

Lo, let that night be solitary, let no joyful voice come therein.

Chapter 12
The Carrot

"If wishes were horses, beggars would ride."

J. Carmichael, "Proverbs in Scot" (1628)

http://news8austin.com/content/your_news?SecID=278&ArID=93453

"My day" occurs tomorrow. I will officially be 43-years-old at 7:39 AM.

When I included the verses from the book of Job, I'd buried my head into the keyboard after slamming my fist into a very expensive computer desk. My oldest son came to console me. He said he was proud of me.

I finally read the Book of Job, ironically in the same spelling as the word for employment, and found it a most depressing book! His friends were despicable! Most of the reading, I felt like physically slapping the TASTE out of their filthy mouths. For Job to pray for the callous snots after their bad advice, even with the Almighty coming to him out of a whirlwind is HERCULEAN to me. Somehow, praying for others makes his circumstances "all better."

Speaking of praying: my wife and I try to pray at 5:00 AM every morning. This is HER idea, mind you. Since God is timeless, and man bound by time, I don't see the difference in giving El Shaddai His due at 6:30 AM after a little more shuteye.

My prayer was testy, angry, blunt, pissed off. Yeah, I was mad at my invisible God. After all, I've been through this Jobian experience for well onto two years. I'm waiting for the whirlwind. I'm tired.

I got a call on my cell. Amazingly, it's the same company that started this Blog in the first place (see the introduction). I don't mention their names as I did there because I don't want to jinx any possibility of getting back into the game.

Peer pressure: it's not just for teenagers. Part of my journey this year was to realize that I am affected by peer pressure. Two instructors I admire are on the cover of Tae Kwon Do Times. They were laid off from their high-tech jobs like me. I had no reason to believe that I could not achieve the same level of success as they did. I was successful in getting the studio as a local interest story on News 8 Austin (see link above). Yet, we don't share the same background, experiences or culture. I can't be like them. I can only be me.

Unfortunately, my net after earnings wasn't and hasn't been much after two years. I made a lot of money and I had to spend a lot of it on advertising and operational costs.

I talked first to the HR rep (a new one!) I talked to an associate of the hiring manager. I talked to THE hiring manager. This was all done as a phone screen. Then, reality set in.

The face-to-face is what I'm waiting on. They didn't actually SAY they were going to pull me in for an interview. This unknown is the biggest problem the unemployed face.

I've been out of the game for two years. I've honorably tried to get a business off the ground to stay in the area. I've honorably looked for other jobs outside of the city and state.

The face-to-face is probably the only answer now I could stand to accept now. My day is tomorrow. My tomorrow is in the balance.

Chapter 13
Surrender

"Neither a borrower nor a lender be;
For loan oft loses both itself and friend,
And borrowing dulls the edge of husbandry.
This above all: to thine own self be true,
And it must follow, as the night the day,
Thou canst not then be false to any man."

William Shakespeare, "Hamlet," Act I, Scene III (Polonius speaking)

Purgatory

By: The Griot Poet

Eye am below Heaven and above hell
Where familiar spirits dwell.

Teased between what appears to be
The "light at the end of the tunnel";
And the licking flames of discontent.

Oldies songs take me back to the seventies:
Before sex;
Before bills;
Before marriage;
Before responsibilities

Eye remember
All eye ever wanted to do was to
Make an honest living.

Somewhere in my story, eye discovered
[John] Milton's nine-level purgatory

Vision... became lust;
"Doing whatever it takes," violating sacred trusts.

If the soul is
The mind,
The will,
The imagination,
The emotions
And the intellect:
Eye sold it!

When do visions become vain imaginations?
When does goal-setting lead to coveting?

Thrust into responsibilities before eye was trained and ready,
Eye skipped down the "Primrose path" -- eye wide shut --

in "no mind,"
Forgetting that
"Action without thought"
Takes prior planning
And much practice.

So, here am eye
At forty-three
Feeling less like
Solomon
And more like
Ecclesiastes *

My prayers as the
Vain repetition
Of a heathen

Teased between what appears to be
The "light at the end of the tunnel";
And the licking flames of discontent.

: Ecclesiastes 1: 2 Vanity of vanities, saith the Preacher, vanity of vanities, all [is] vanity.

My alter ego revealed.

I originally wanted to title this chapter "Bankruptcy," since that option is on my mind, and the rules for it will change by October after the end of the fiscal year.

I've been on a two-year journey. I've documented the pains I've felt, the self-doubt, the despair, and the hopes.

This is a process, long, complicated.

I remember a video I saw of Charles Dickens in a class based on Steven Covey's "The Seven Habits of Highly Effective People." He was despondent, depressed walking through the despair of the streets of London in an economic depression -- with no story idea. For most of us that viewed it with hindsight -- I was sitting next to a very good friend that was up on her literature -- we recognized the beginning of the plot for "A Tale of Two Cities": *It was the best of times; it was the worst of times.*

That kind of recognition -- the Zen balance of life -- is where I am now.

My emotions, and granted, I've been in touch with some I initially put away on a dark, machismo shelf for many years -- are validated.

My hopes for a better tomorrow are justified.

And my desire for meaning of this crazy phase of my life is "vanity." Other translations say: "Everything is meaningless," says the Teacher, "utterly meaningless!"

The job I thought I wanted at the company I had an HR rep for is in a hiring freeze until early next year.

The job that started this blog called me -- twice -- and it looks good. My hope.

I surrender to the understanding of life. "For in much wisdom [is] much grief: and he that increases knowledge increases sorrow." Eccl 1:18

I surrender to the seasons that must process through my life: "To every [thing there is] a season, and a time to every purpose under the heaven": Eccl 3:1.

Seasons change every ninety days. I look forward to my time to heal, my time to laugh, and my time to dance!

(Eccl 3:3&4 [paraphrased])

Chapter 14
Sighs, Brass and Tinkling Symbols

"The soul that is within me no man can degrade."

Frederick Douglas

From the Introduction (see archives for 2004):

11/23/2004

HR's reply:

You are on the hiring managers list of calls to make - I looked at the tracking sheet this AM.

(Name blanked out)

*****

My (14 August) e-mail:

I've talked to --- and ------ regarding the opportunity. I am confident we had good rapport and exchanged pertinent information on the position and its expectations. I am motivated to take the next step in this opportunity! I look forward to your reply to this e-mail, or call me at --------.

Thank you, and best regards,
Reggie Goodwin

*****

(New) HR's reply:

Hi Reggie…I don't have an answer for you yet. As soon as I do I will let you know.

Thanks,

*****

"Though I speak with the tongues of men and of angels, and have not charity, I am become [as] sounding brass, or a tinkling cymbal." 1 Cor 13:1.

Sounds of sighing are
Like unto the sound of one
Hand clapping: hopeful.

Though I could have said "hopeless," I chose the word because the syllables match the beat of a proper haiku. Also, with a single word, the mood of the poem changes from somber to bright.

An extension of charity from a friend:

"Happy belated birthday Reggie! I love Ecclesiastes, and the book of Jude is also a favorite of mine. I studied End Time Bible prophecy with a minister who travels the world doing seminars on that subject (Larry Wilson) for 6 years every day ... then I wrote a book, 'Thy Kingdom Come', that sold out in the Family Christian Store. I'd change some of it now, but it was pretty good I think.

"If we're well into the time of the end (I think we are), God would take you out of the 'system' for your own protection Reggie ... at just about this point.

"I took myself out of the system, some time ago because that's going to be important. In the spring, I'm going to be planting a huge garden, wildflowers, then flowering plants and bushes, veggies, and herbs. I'm just feeling lead to do that. It's going to be important now, to be spirit-led, Reggie.

"If you have time and you're interested, it might be worthwhile for you to look into Mayan prophecy, Native American prophecy, Tibetan Prophecy, Celestine Prophecy, the Dead Sea Scrolls are also worth looking into the (Essences scriptures). Know what? It's possible that you're more like Saul than Job ... Paul was caught up in the world that he was living in, until God separated him and taught him, in the desert. God saw something special in Paul. There are supposed to be prophets prepared for this time ... "God never does anything without first informing his servants, the prophets" You never know. Know what book I love, I have "A guide to the I Ching", I just read it like a book of philosophy, it's really inspirational.

"I love all the Epistles, Paul seems so human to me. Some of your writing sounds like him.... "What I would do, I do not" etc.

"Keep on Reggie, Love, --------"

Out of respect for the poet's privacy, I've omitted her name.

My homeboy, Ivanhoe, says poets are Prophets Of Eternal Truths.

If I am a prophet, this time of my life is my desert.

I am pleased that what I've written has touched at least one. I hope it has touched you.

I am wretched. I struggle with inner demons. I am all-together human.

Although, I wryly observe, beheading is "in vogue" again, and I remember that was Paul's demise at the hands of the Roman government. Also, due to being left for dead, shipwrecked and the infamous "thorn," I hope the Apostle and I only share writing styles and philosophical outlook.

My... a funny! I believe I am... choosing joy.

Chapter 15
Once More… Into the Breach

"Once more unto the breach, dear friends, once more;
Or close the wall up with our English dead."

William Shakespeare, "Henry V, Act III, Scene I"

http://www-tech.mit.edu/Shakespeare/works.html

[HR rep],

I received your e-mail yesterday. I will be patient.
Could I possibly receive addresses for ------ and ---? I'd like to send them thank you letters.

Regards,
Reggie Goodwin

*****

Hi Reggie…Thanks for your patience. I'm afraid we are at a standstill at the moment, there is some internal reshuffling going on in this department at the moment, so we cannot make any decisions about hiring. I hope to know something for you in a few days or maybe by this time next week. If you do not hear from me sooner, feel free to check back with me this time next week.

Thanks again for your time and patience, I understand it's frustrating not to have an answer.

*****

[HR rep],

Whatever your internal reshuffling, I'd still like to thank them personally. If you have a policy against it, I'll understand. I thought it the professional response to the phone screens.

Reggie

"Once more unto the breach, dear friends, once more;
"Or close the wall up with our English dead.
"In peace there's nothing so becomes a man
"As modest stillness and humility:
"But when the blast of war blows in our ears,
"Then imitate the action of the tiger;
"Stiffen the sinews, summon up the blood,
"Disguise fair nature with hard-favour'd rage;..."

William Shakespeare, Henry V, Act III, Scene I

Chapter 16
On Faith

"Now faith is the substance of things hoped for,
the evidence of things not seen."

Hebrews 11: 1

A particularly nerdy essay I apparently wrote to... myself.

On Faith

Hebrews 11: 1 "Now faith is the substance of things hoped for, the evidence of things not seen."

A moderately skilled logician would render the previous word problem thusly:

Faith = null + null.

Null, according to Webster, functions as an adjective, as in "null set." It connotes "having no legal or binding force, invalid"; "amounting to nothing, nil"; "having no value, insignificant."

The Apostle Paul is quoted often in sermons and motivational lectures without the impact of his statement clearly understood in the current lexicon. Further analysis from Webster also states null as "having no elements, mathematically, a null set." In the refrain of a seventies song I recall with fondness: *"Nothing plus nothing leaves nothing. [And] you got to have something if you want to be with me."*

Since physics jobs are testily unavailable to undergraduate degreed applicants, and engineering pays better, the following definition caught my fancy: "null is a measurement in which an unknown quantity (as of electric current) is compared with a known quantity of the same kind and found equal by a null detector."

The problem that Paul introduces is in his formula for faith, without which, it is impossible to please God.

THE UNKNOWN GOD

What is unique about the Hebrews of early Palestine was the lack of representation of a physical body in art. Moses, the lawgiver, whose gravesite is purported to be Mount Nebo in Jordan (See "The Memorial of Moses at Mount Nebo, ***http://198.62.75.1/www1/ofm/***

fai/FAInebo1.html), made the stipulation for the early believers that they construct "no graven images." This influenced Hebrew artists until after about the 10th century AD when they began to depict the human body, and the first earliest physical descriptions of what they looked like.

Europe and literally the entire known kingdoms of the earth at that time did not share this peculiarity. Their gods had physical, human forms, beautiful and handsome. The gods had specific functions they carried out in their respective pantheon (notably the Egyptians, Greeks, Norwegians, and Romans gods bore striking resemblance in their functionality). There were gods of the rain, wind, frost, mist, water, thunder, love, war, and harvest. Their gods had sex with each other and humans. Their gods became jealous and had wars. They demanded ritual sacrifice of bullocks and lambs at their altars: some sects also sacrificed humans.

The Hebrew God had no form. He demanded devotion, characteristically of the other gods with ritual sacrifice, but called for no human sacrifice save twice in written text.

"What proof do I have that God exists?" None… null… nada… zero.

Scientific method dictates "Principles and procedures for the systematic pursuit of knowledge involving the recognition and formulation of a problem, the collection of data through observation and experiment, and the formulation and testing of hypotheses." (From Webster.) Interestingly, the phrase came into usage in 1854; its Etymology is Greek, from hypotithenai to put under, suppose, from hypo- + tithenai to put (circa 1656).

All that to say, I'd have to put God in a test tube; pour into a crucible, break down by way of some decomposition experiment and evaluate the discrete parts. That would not be deity: it would be an element on the periodic table.

Related to the Scientific Method are tools utilized to reach conclusions: hypothesis, theory, and law.

HYPOTHESIS implies insufficient evidence to provide more than a tentative explanation, e.g. a hypothesis explaining the extinction of the dinosaurs.

THEORY implies a greater range of evidence and greater likelihood of truth, e.g. the theory of evolution.

LAW implies a statement of order and relation in nature that has been found to be invariable under the same conditions, e.g. the law of gravitation.

Acts 17: 18, 22 – 23

"Then certain philosophers of the Epicureans, and of the Stoics, encountered him. And some said, what will this babbler say? Others say, he seems to be a setter forth of strange gods: because he preached unto them Jesus, and the resurrection.

"Then Paul stood in the midst of Mars' hill, and said, [You] men of Athens, I perceive that in all things you are too superstitious.

"For as I passed by, and beheld your devotions, I found an altar with this inscription, TO THE UNKNOWN GOD. Whom therefore you ignorantly worship, Him I declare unto you."

This is a lively chapter. Paul, after having turned the city upside down, according to the Judaic factions there debated the key philosophers of the day.

Epicures lived between 341 – 270 BC, a Greek philosopher who taught that "pleasure is the only good and the end of all morality, through a life of simplicity, prudence, honor, and justice." He's best remembered in the phrase "eat, drink, and be merry." (A real party animal.)

Stoics were members of a school of philosophy founded by Zeno of Citium about 300 BC holding that "the wise man should be free from passion, unmoved by joy or grief, and submissive to natural law;

one apparently or professedly indifferent to pleasure or pain." (For all you Trekkers out there, this is the inspiration and job description of Mr. Spock.)

Verses 29 & 32:

"Forasmuch then as we are the offspring of God, we ought not to think that the Godhead is like unto gold, or silver, or stone, graven by art and man's device.

"And when they heard of the resurrection of the dead, some mocked: and others said, we will hear thee again of this [matter]," after which, Paul leaves.

Poverty and the 1st Null set

"Now faith is the substance of things hoped for…"

I am not a rich man. I grew up lower middle class in a segregated neighborhood of the segregated South in North Carolina. Forced bussing introduced me to light brown skin, blond, brunette, and redhead friends. I met my share of rednecks, too.

Modern day Epicureans, in my estimation, are probably not hungry. That which they conceive they and their lofty American and Swiss bank accounts can achieve.

Conception would be an inhibitor to conversation with such an individual(s). If you cannot conceive living a poor existence, you tend not to look at systems in effect for centuries, oversights of human government, or just plain bad luck. Such a person would probably blame the individual in the impoverished situation. They'd be right part of the time, but not all. Until they've hoped for their next meal, prayed for a sick child, found that their wealth couldn't address the most perplex of human issues – death – they wouldn't get it because they wouldn't have to. They would consider me, as Paul, a babbler.

Schrödinger's cat and the 2nd Null set

"...The evidence of things not seen."

Erin Schrödinger is best known for an equation that describes the wave nature of elementary particles, and is fundamental to the description of the properties of all matter. Sometimes referred to as particle/wave duality: it is the basis for the branch of physics known as Quantum Mechanics.

To illustrate this, Schrödinger used a technique called a Gedankin, German for "thought experiment." Here, in a nutshell, it is thus:

"If you place a cat in a perfectly sealed box and break a bottle of Radium with a remote trigger device, is the cat living or dead?"

Most would say, "it depends on the amount of Radium"; or "it depends on the time of exposure." Erin probably didn't intentionally want to anger any animal rights activists. Remember that this was all in his head.

The answer in Quantum Mechanics is "both," i.e. the cat is living and dead until the reality of its fate is substantiated by an observer.

For our Stoic/Mr. Spock mentality, "this is not logical." Such illogic, such uncertainty is the realm of Quantum Physics. Light can be observed as a photon or a wave. Electrical energy can be observed as an electron or [radio] waves. The perspective is based upon the observer, or witness. S/He reaches their own conclusion based on their own...faith.

A [paraphrased] joke from my former pastor:

"A believer lived next door to an atheist. She was a poor woman without money. Nightly, she prayed for food from God. The atheist, ever eager to prove his point bought the woman food. She began to shout for joy, praising God. The atheist triumphantly entered her apartment saying 'you see? God does not exist. God didn't buy you those groceries. I did!'

“She praised louder and longer. ‘Didn’t you hear me, you silly woman? God didn’t buy you those groceries, I did!’

“She looked at the atheist and said ‘God not only provided groceries, he made the devil pay for them!’”

“Human existence in the saga of the cosmos can only be explained as an act of a God who intended to create beings like us.” Stephen Hawkings, Nobel Laureate Physicist, “A Brief History of Time.”

Chapter 17
Full Circle

"One ought, every day at least, to hear a little song,
read a good poem, see a fine picture, and if it were
possible to speak a few reasonable words in order
that worldly cares may not obliterate the sense
of the beautiful which God has
implanted in the human soul."

Johann von Goethe

http://www.bls.gov

Hi Reggie,

I want to take a moment to thank you for your interest in -------. While your past skills and experience are impressive, we didn't feel there was a strong fit for our current opening.

I enjoyed talking with you and want to thank you for the time you spent with us and for your interest in the position. Please feel free to watch our careers page and apply if something in your interest area opens up.

Thanks again and good luck in your search.

Sincerely,

[HR rep]

*****

My reply:

Thank you, -----.

I have updated my profile in your database.

{To anonymous -- an announcement to you, not the HR rep}

*****

I have had the most amazing conversations with men.

I am now 43 years old. "While my past skills and experience are impressive, no one seems to feel they are a strong fit for their current opening."

I am fine.

I've talked to men about my age and predicament. One has a web design business. From time-to-time he goes for interviews -- mostly for the fun of it -- passes their written examinations and their verbal queries. Yet, "though his skills and experience are impressive..." they hire "Joe College."

I am fine.

I talk to men that are in the same predicament. We have past skills that are impressive, or we're overqualified "based on our years of experience."

I am fine.

What's interesting about our conversations is that we have the same fears, the same self-doubts, the same prayers unanswered. We have the same hopes, the same dreams, and the same aspirations -- to feed and provide for our households.

I am F.I.N.E.

But here, the acronym does not mean "**F**reaked out, **I**rritated, **N**eurotic, and **E**rratic." At the beginning of the blog, I admit it probably did.

I have lived beyond severance, beyond benefits, beyond unemployment checks. I've managed to survive a semester at the University of Texas, Austin in Astronomy. I'm going back in the fall for two classes and a project with youth at middle and high schools. I've commented in two women's books: "Life is a Song Worth Singing" (poetry) and "Secret Sins of the Heart" (memoir) by Clarissa Bolding and Rachel Caron. I'm working on the commentary for a good friend, Joe Brundidge on his book of poems "The Naked Truth of Element 615" (his stage name). I have enrolled in a copywriting course that apparently came at the right time.

I take no credit for the above blessings, for these blessings are from Above.

So, I am F.I.N.E.: **F**ired up, **I**nspired, **N**aturally talented, and **E**cstatic.

I realize that I have the right to control what something means.

So, as an act of faith and not of vengeance, I am pulling my resume from all sites: Monster, Hot Jobs, Drake Beam Morin and specific company alerts. This should please the Bureau of Labor Statistics: the unemployment rate is only tabulated for the persons receiving benefits. In an Orwellian sense, I have voluntarily become an "un-person."

I will not apply for or receive unemployment benefits. I will live by my talents and live well.

My past skills and experiences are impressive, and those that feel I am not a strong fit for their organization will soon see what they have lost. The fact is they cannot pay me the amount I am truly worth. **I AM** priceless.

Chapter 18
Invictus' Anniversary

"Under the bludgeoning of chance
My head is bloody, but unbowed."

William Ernst Hensley, "Invictus"

All honor to my noble brothers worldwide of Kappa Alpha Psi Fraternity, Inc.

<u>Invictus</u>

(William Ernest Henley 1849 - 1903)

OUT of the night that covers me,
Black as the Pit from pole to pole
I thank whatever gods may be
For my unconquerable soul.

In the fell clutch of circumstance
I have not winced nor cried aloud.
Under the bludgeoning of chance
My head is bloody, but unbowed.

Beyond this place of wrath and tears
Looms but the Horror of the shade,
And yet, the menace of the years
Finds, and shall find, me unafraid.

It matters not how strait the gate
How charged with punishment the SCROLL,
I am the master of my fate:
I am the captain of my soul.

*****

<u>Son of Invictus</u>

By: The Griot Poet

I am Invictus!

"My head is bloody, [yet] unbowed."
Two years removed from the game by

Downsizing,
Rightsizing,
Outsourcing

Have only revealed that I AM the source
Of my reality;

I AM the cause of my destruction or salvation.

I don't have to look beyond my own faith to know
"every need is met"

Because
I AM!

Controlling what something means:

"They don't want me."
Who needs them?

"They don't want to pay me."
They can't afford me!

"I am out of work."
I am OFF the Silicon plantation and ***done*** *with sharecropping my gifts.*

"I am unemployed."
I am free to explore and use my talents in a way that pleases me, and the God that I believe in.

I am free to grieve on this anniversary of my father's death (six years ago) and my demise from Corporate America (two years ago) on this date. Or, I can control what this means... and move on with my life.

Chapter 19
Open Letter

“Live as if you were to die tomorrow.
Learn as if you were to live forever.”

Mahatma Gandhi

An Open Letter To:
The President of the United States
The Senate and the Congress

Dear Sir, Sirs and Madams:

I am an outsourced American.

The previous blog chapters you've read have been rants, rages, prayers and praises, celebrations and lamentations. I've meant no harm to myself, my family or to any representative of any corporation.

However, I feel I have a right to my freedom of speech. Lay offs, downsizing and outsourcing has attached to it human emotions, human families, dwindling bank accounts and diminishing American dreams.

"What happens to a dream deferred?
"Does it dry up like a raisin in the sun?
"Or, fester like a sore and then run?"

Langston Hughes, Dream Deferred

I am an American of African decent; my last name given to my paternal great-grandmother and grandfather Epsy and Julius Goodwin on their freedom from slavery in 1865.

I grew up in a ghetto, east of the demarcation of Winston-Salem, North Carolina, US 52. I saw drug deals, prostitutes and lived next to addicts of various stripes.

I achieved a degree in Engineering Physics at North Carolina Agricultural and Technical State University. Jesse Jackson, Jesse Jackson Jr., Dr. Ronald E. McNair (deceased: the Challenger accident) are a few of its noteworthy graduates.

I was a commissioned officer in the United States Air Force. My specialty was communications. After serving four years, I went to graduate school briefly at Texas State in San Marcos and was employed in the Semiconductor Industry at a major company in Austin, Texas.

I was laid off 26 August 2003 on the fourth anniversary of my father's death. I have observed the passing of my second anniversary as an outsourced American.

By the sheer grace of God, I am in graduate school at the University of Texas, Austin in Astronomy. I am retraining. I will still be an advocate for the American science and engineering professional when my education is completed.

I refer to myself as an outsourced American. My story is beyond party affiliations and beyond racial ethnicities.

You are all currently grappling with matters of life-and-death in the aftermath of hurricane Katrina and the hundreds, soon thousands lost in Louisiana and Mississippi. My cousin lived in New Orleans, Louisiana. Luckily, he was north of New Orleans, visiting his daughter and son-in-law. His home is gone. My first apartment used to be in Biloxi, Mississippi. I called it my "two step" apartment: I could take approximately two steps from the bedroom to the bathroom, two from the bedroom to the kitchen and two from the bedroom to the living room! It is also a pleasant, washed away memory. I see the myriad faces of people on the news, looting or surviving, depending on your point of view. Two-thirds of which are African American that look like my relatives; that look like me.

I call your attention, in the days and weeks ahead, to the American worker. The unemployment rate is today 4.9%, but that is a misnomer: it does not count me. Nor does it count those others like me dropped from the unemployment roll after exhausting their benefits and no longer receiving a bi-monthly check. It does not count the victims of the current ecological disaster. October's unemployment figure should be interesting indeed.

Every pundit and lobbyist, every accountant and economist, defends outsourcing: the observation is, pundits and economists positions are ***not*** threatened by the maneuver.

I am not an accountant nor am I an economist. I do make these observations:

- The University of Texas, Austin reports a decrease in the number of engineering undergraduate students. This trend is probably observable from other flagship and minor colleges and universities around the nation. Young people are not going to invest the time and considerable labor in the attainment of a science and engineering degree if there are no viable jobs to matriculate to after graduation.

- As a former child of the ghetto, I can attest that if you provide the excitement of science and engineering training and the youth have the talent and time to grasp it, they will make positive, life-affirming choices that only better American society.

- Our universities will become revolving doors: foreign exchange students, welcome at all times, will matriculate and attain degrees, then go back to their host countries. If there are no jobs here, there is no need to stay. Diversity in the workplace will eventually devolve to pre 1965 levels.

- If you continue outsourcing American professional and technical jobs, the next innovations will come from overseas. That cannot be good for our national security, since we will not be in proximity to protect any trade secrets.

- If you continue outsourcing science, engineering, manufacturing and technician level jobs, the middle class will eventually shrink. There will be no "bootstrap self-lift" from poverty, into middle class and upper middle class: that can only be bridged by continuing education.

- The American economy is based on the collection of an income tax. Many government and military programs are financed by this method. If jobs are outsourced to India and China because the professionals there can do the same jobs for approximately $5,000.00 per year, we cannot gather a tax from them, as they are not citizens of this nation.

- My income for the last two years has been a declining negative. Therefore, I cannot be taxed at the bracket I once occupied. Furthermore, my charitable giving to churches and causes like the relief efforts for hurricane Katrina are hampered. I'd give if I only had. Right now, I can give my prayers, some canned goods and my time.

I hope in future legislations, sessions of Congress and the Senate, passage of bills that the persons you think about are not just corporations and their profits, but of *"We the People, of the United States, in order to form a more perfect union, establish justice, insure domestic tranquility. Provide for the common defense, promote the general welfare, and to secure the blessing of liberty to ourselves and our posterity, do ordain and establish this constitution of the United States of America."*

I thank you, Sir, Sirs, and Madams for your time.

Sincerely,

Reginald L. Goodwin,
Outsourced American

Chapter 20
Epilogue

"Nine requisites for contented living:
Health enough to make work a pleasure;
Wealth enough to support your needs;
Strength to battle with difficulties and overcome them;
Grace enough to confess your sins and forsake them.
Patience enough to toil until some good is accomplished;
Charity enough to see some good in your neighbor,
Love enough to move you to be useful and helpful to others.
Faith enough to make real the things of God;
Hope enough to remove all anxious fears
concerning the future."

Johann Von Goethe

I chose this chapter to summarize my journey.

What I've left are "spiritual bread crumbs."

In my post on ***http://griotpoet.blogspot.com*** 19 November 2004, I left this sad news:

In memoriam: This is from a friend and fellow poet, Ron Horne about the passage of a light in poetry, Ana Rose, also known as Phoenix. This touched me because we don't talk about depression. I'm old enough to remember Donnie Hathaway (R&B singer, Roberta Flack duets) and his similar demise.

We don't as a culture like to talk about depression or suicide. It's unfortunate that many creative types like Donnie Hathaway, Curt Cobain (Nirvana) and Phoenix feel that they have no hope when their words have given people so many memories; so much to live for.

A reminder: give your flowers to your friends in THIS life!

My Brothers and Sisters in Poetry-

The news filtered up to me here in Austin that a Sun Poet, Ana Rose, aka Phoenix, took her life on Friday, leaping from the roof of an office building in San Antonio. Phoenix was a young woman, 30 years old or so, bright, bubbling, full of life and always out supporting both poets and musicians. She could be found at poetry venues and band gigs throughout San Antonio as well as on the road. She was a kind and caring spirit.

In her wake are the common questions: why did she do it, who knew she was that desperate, if I had only known, if I only had . . . . There are probably many things many of us could have done, but without really knowing her strife, there is little any one could have done . . . However, as members of a very unique family, the family of poetry and verse, we could have spoken to her, and others like her, both directly and through our art, to let her know that we have ALL been in desperate situations and that there is ALWAYS someone to turn to, even if only for a moment. The closeness and support we have in the poetry community is tighter than some people have in their biological families. We have the unique ability to reach out through our art to touch those around us, to let them know that as bad as it may seem, the beauty of what we do can bring something positive to their lives.

It pains me to know this young life was lost in despair. None of us are mind readers so there is only so much we can do. But let's try to remind each other as often as we can that every time a day ends, on the next day new life begins. With that, I present two poems in honor of the Phoenix; may her spirit arise in all of us. I send this to you in the hope that between all of us, wherever we are, we don't let another bird of paradise get away:

FLIGHT OF THE PHOENIX

They say that every Phoenix rises
But when life provides no compromises
It should come as no surprise
That a Phoenix is nothing more . . . than a sparrow
Seeking crumbs on narrow streets
Flying from the tip of tall buildings
To the hard concrete
Succumb to defeat
Rather than suffer the constant struggle

The battle of tug of war
Is just a metaphor
Where there can only be one winner
The kind and compassionate
Are the perpetually condemned sinners
Heartache the blood thinner
That turns cool breezes into artic winds
Causes a young life to rescind
Her covenant with her glory

To hear she took her life
Tore me and all that knew her apart
Didn't she know that the community of art
And love covet her departure?
Because now only the angels will know
Why the Phoenix flew away

Ron Horne

*****

<u>I KNEW HER AS ROSE</u>

She came to be known as Phoenix
But I first knew her as Rose
And little did I know
That she was in the throes
Of a struggle with life and death

So on that humid August night
As we all skinny dipped
How could I know that in her mind
The scales would tip
And she would slip
Down a slope
That at its depth lacked the hope
She needed to keep going

How could I know that
As she placed her tiny hand in mine
The cosmic design
Had a disturbing fate in place
Where she paced back and forth
Between the door to existence
And the door to extinction
To learn that she found not distinction
Between the two

Leaves me to ponder
My own bouts with suicidal ideation
Those times where I lamented whether
My own creation was a mistake
Ready to preclude another candle
Impaling my birthday cake
Break the cycle of constant misery
That seemed to plague me daily
Yes, if it weren't for poetry
I would have missed the gallantry
Of my son's well and hard fought triumphs
I would have forgotten the fact that it is enough
To be loved without necessarily being the beloved
That the joy of life is toughing it out
Long enough to see the BIG picture

So, as the regret flows
The fire in me grows
To spend life on my tip toes
Reaching for the light that glows
She came to be know as Phoenix
But to me, she was a perennial Rose

Ron Horne

*****

Thanks, Ron.

So, my motivation was more self-preservation than literary acclaim. I left "spiritual bread crumbs" to others that otherwise would not have e-mailed, called, stopped me in hallways or contacted me in anyway.

It is sad that in a world of over six billion people, we can feel we're all alone. We can feel isolated and aloof. That is when the mind plays tricks on you; the "fiery darts of the enemy" plants the seeds of your own destruction with justifiable reasons to accomplish the sordid deed.

I hope this frankness; this open honesty has helped others in similar situations. Blogging has helped me get through this phase of my life. Perhaps your method is painting. Perhaps you method is sculpture or poetry. It does not matter. Leave "spiritual bread crumbs"; let people that know you know how you're feeling. Get in touch with your feelings through a therapist or clergy. Get angry, express it and get over it. Get out and live life again! Isolation is the road to destruction. You **do** matter!

*****

Now, my apologies… I feel a need to apologize for forgiveness, and to forgive.

I've been reading a fascinating book called "Blue Like Jazz: Nonreligious Thoughts on Christian Spirituality," by Donald Miller (***www.bluelikejazz.com***). The back cover reads: *"I never liked jazz because jazz music doesn't resolve. But sometimes you have to watch someone love something before you can love it yourself… I used to not like God because God didn't resolve. But that was before any of this happened…" He also has a statement in the front cover that grabbed me: "In America, the first generation out of slavery invented jazz music. It is a free-form expression. It comes from the soul, and it is true."*

Jazz. Euphemism for sex, it is an original art form from the Mississippi delta and New Orleans (sadly, now underwater). It is jambalaya, crawdads and etouffée. Like spoken word poetry, it does not traditionally follow a pattern. To the chagrin of classical musical artists, it does not resolve. Neither does the mystery of life on the edge of ruin. It puts the formula "now faith is the substance of things hoped for; the evidence of things not seen" into perspective.

My first apology: to the subjects of my article "My Encounter With Black Republicans," published in The Creative Pulse of Austin Magazine.

Dear Sirs:

Though I did not receive any monetary gain for the article, I did receive a level of satisfaction at the typing of it. I made you look like buffoons and idiots. I apologize for being as woefully guilty of the ignorance you demonstrated.

Though one of you is from America and the other from Nigeria, you are entitled to your political opinions, as am I. The argument between us only started with my identifying myself as a poet. That labeled me (from the African American gentleman) as a "Bush Hater," which was to suggest that every poet is.

You'll be happy to know that my republican poet friends were not too happy at your broad brush. Many of them thought you hadn't been republican long enough to have such strong opinions. Others expressed themselves in language that I'd prefer not to repeat in this blog. (Just look at anything Mark Twain said or wrote when he was mad. His and their comments are laced with most *colorful* metaphors!)

For the record: I am a pragmatist, neither republican, democrat, green, libertarian or reform party. Radically and metaphorically, I am the whip in the hand of Christ as he chased the moneychangers out of the temple, hence my engagement with you since I detest dogma over spirit and truth. I choose the candidates I vote for from the information I can research and I'm given. I also choose them based on my conscience and how I live with the decisions I make, as do you.

And my sincerest apologies for calling you black republicans. The Nigerian gentleman does not have citizenship, so this last election is one of many he did not voice his opinion in, nor can he. The African American gentleman's father seems to be a staunch democrat from comments I've heard about him. I doubt he challenges his father's beliefs because he has a vested interest in their continued relationship as father and son. He is blessed to still have his in this life.

I was extremely angry with you both drawing my wife into the argument culminated. I did something irrational and dangerous at the dinner party: I deployed my "Night Stalker," but you didn't seem to notice. I'll explain.

The Night Stalker is a model of knives sold by Cold Steel ®. I carried it in my pocket as I usually do. It's within the Texas legal limit of 4", non-serrated for personal protection. It can stand up to two hundred pounds of pressure on its hinge joint, and I am an expert with it. However, you did not threaten me physically. As a martial artist, I must feel myself under threat of assault with intent to harm before I can use any amount of force. And with twenty-seven years of martial arts experience, no amount of clever arguments could have halted a massacre. It makes me shudder to think about it!

However, you intentionally involved my wife in your diatribe. I've raised two wonderful sons with her that, despite my current financial state still respect me and love me as father and husband. My anger seethed from this emotional attachment. Also, I never have nor will I ever say anything negative about your wives to either of you.

I was also angry because I'd just started this journey (you might be reading about here) as an outsourced American. I was disoriented. I was hurt. I was angry with a company and industry I'd given so much time to, so much talent to, so much energy to jettisoning me like so much garbage! People who looked like me and attacked with such impunity, such a freedom I know you would not exercise at your respective workplaces. Also, I'm not the kind to strike a man when he's down… as you did me.

For that, I forgive you.

*****

My second apology: to the company and industry that laid me off, rejected my resumes and got my hopes up with dangled carrots.

To Whom It May Concern:

First of all, the semiconductor industry started with the invention of the transistor, or "trans resistor" from the genius of William Shockley (see: junction transistor, Shockley Diode Equation, 1952). Of course, this could not have begun without the amplified vacuum tube (Lee de Forest, 1912); ENIAC: the Electronic Numerical Integrator and Computer (1943, one BIG mother). Jack Kilby pioneered a method of stacking different types of semiconductors together in 1958 giving us the precursor to our modern processing recipe steps. Jean Hoerni invented the planar transistor in 1959. Also that year, Robert Noyce innovated from connecting wires to "conduction channels" patterned on wafers with photolithography and etched into the underlying Aluminum (some copper and gold for conduction) metal layer. Robert Noyce was a cofounder of Fairchild Semiconductor and Intel. *

I said William Shockley for a reason: he was known for a mercurial management style and his unscientific beliefs in Eugenics, i.e. his racial superiority and my culture's racial inferiority. +

There was a spirit of that evident when I worked in the industry, largely because of the effort made to define diversity, a subset of Affirmative Action that soon included every group that ever felt discriminated against, soon to include Llama and Malamute Lovers. It was also evident in my promotion cycles (or, lack thereof); the papers I published that received no recognition of technical excellence; the differential treatment of one coworker who was frankly, a constant "screw up" that was tolerated; another who on the first night shift at my former employer announced to everyone on the production floor his wife was a "b----": they promoted him to management.

: Jeffrey R. Rodengen, "The Spirit of AMD (Advanced Micro Devices), © 1998, pp 13 – 15; 16 – 18. +: Shockley, William. Shockley on Eugenics and Race: The Application of Science to the Solution of Human Problems. Pearson, Roger, ed. Washington: Scott-Townsend Publishers, 1992. 292 p.

It is thanks to the science of Genetics, the Human Genome Diversity project found genetic commonalities with some Anglo Americans and Australian aborigines. As they searched countless strands of DNA, they could find nothing that called one person or group "superior" or the other "inferior." They did find we all have a common genetic ancestor on the continent of Africa. We're all "soul brothers" at the root, I'm afraid.

I said all that to say this: think about what you want to produce in the outcome of the global marketplace. Is it that easy to shift professional jobs overseas? What about using your resources to build up the infrastructure of the inner cities and pull from a talent pool that 1) doesn't look like you; 2) are from a different culture? Shipping our jobs overseas only allows you to pull from a talent pool that 1) doesn't look like you; 2) are from a different culture and 3) do not pay income taxes here. All you'll have is a revolving door of talent going to our universities and leaving for home. What about the students here that want to make a professional living, BUY the products that they're responsible for producing and support the nation with their income taxes paid? What about the middle class? For that matter, who's going to replace the professors at the colleges when they get too old to teach and retire? Remember, what you do to one American will eventually be done to you.

For that, I forgive you.

*****

My third apology: to the headhunters and HR managers that dangled carrots.

I use the metaphor "dangled carrots" again for a reason.

You are the first line of contact with any corporation I've ever worked for or ever applied to.

I remember when you were "Personnel" before you became "Human Resource Management." As I define each word through Webster:

<u>Human:</u> a: having human form or attributes **b:** susceptible to or representative of the sympathies and frailties of human nature <such an inconsistency is very *human*>

<u>Resource:</u> 1 a: a source of supply or support: an available means -- usually used in plural **b:** a natural source of wealth or revenue -- often used in plural, an ability to meet and handle a situation

<u>Management:</u> 1: the act or art of managing: the conducting or supervising of something (as a business), **2:** judicious use of means to accomplish an end, **3:** the collective body of those who manage or direct an enterprise

You therefore, fall under rules of engagement that put you in particularly delicate situations. When all is well with the economy, rejection only means, "move on to the next opportunity." When it is not, the subjects you contact are "susceptible to or representative of the sympathies and frailties of human nature." Hence, my rants, which I sincerely doubt are new to you at all.

There must be a win-win engagement strategy for future attempts at sourcing a talent pool. There must be some method of suggesting if not now, how can we present ourselves better in the future? It would eliminate a waste of precious time for both parties involved.

I've heard that my resume presents too much "life experience" (we can't say I'm old) that you're not apt to look at or pay for. So, are we at the HR equivalent of "Logan' Run"? (See: "Finished At Forty," ***http://www.fortune.com/fortune/articles/0,15114,375941,00.html***) Are we putting the American worker out to pasture because companies don't want to pay for their experience? What then is the motivation to get the experience, to matriculate to your companies, to work at all? These are things you have to think long and hard about.

Don't allow bureaucracy to tie your hands. As with hurricane Katrina, the time to think about what to do should not be in the hindsight of the storm that blew through.

For that, I forgive you.

My fourth apology: to Bobby R. Taylor, attorney

Dear Sir:

I apologize for monopolizing your time with trivial matters. However, you will hopefully understand, I don't see my livelihood and my ability to care for and provide for my family as trivial.

I only wish I'd met you as a younger, idealistic lawyer when the fire to "fight the good fight" was still hot in you.

I was looking for a crusader. You've obviously built a comfortable living around winnable cases and not on the underdog.

Your name is the one that came up as you advertise on a community radio station in Austin, KAZI-FM. You've obviously had many dealings with then in the recent past: in your lobby I saw a poem written to you by Reverend Frank Garrett, Jr. of "The Wake Up Call," a program on which I heard your advertisement, jazz background music and all. Hence, you were the first lawyer that came to mind. I cannot dictate your criterion for taking on caseloads.

For that, I forgive you.

*****

My last apology: living a lie of faith.

When things are fine and food is plentiful; when you have every need met at the end of a credit statement paid on time; when you can go on any plane to anywhere you imagine without fear of a terrorist attack; when gas is $0.98 per gallon it's easy to have faith. Life resolves like a stanza of Beethoven's ninth symphony. It is beautiful.

When things are crazy and food is scarce; when you've blown out every credit extended you; when your eighty-year-old mother falls and you are finagling a means to go see her; when gas is $3.00 a gallon, faith is a challenge. You curse a lot more than you'd like to. Life sounds like acid rock reverberating off a dry chalkboard being scratched. It is ugly!

"Now, faith is the substance of things hoped for; the evidence of things not seen." And the physical church is just a building, a classroom where you get your nourishment. For some, it's poetry readings; for other's it's a temple or meditation in a forest. The real body – ecclesia – is me. This is what it is for me. Thus, the substance of things hoped for are my expectations.

So, in the midst of this "faith fight," I choose to change my expectations. It does not resolve. But it is from *my* soul. And, it is true.

For that, I forgive ME!

Acknowledgements

To my family: Mildred D. Goodwin, Robert H. Goodwin (deceased), my sister Mamie G. Douglas, my wife Cassandra L. Goodwin, my sons, Robbin R. Collins and Jonathan A. Goodwin; my mother-in-law Anne Williams and many cousins, brothers and sisters-in-laws. You believed in my goals and nurtured my dreams both educationally and financially. You are the first evidence of the providence and love of God in my life. I thank you.

To Doctors I.V. and Bridget Hilliard; Pastor Ed and Vickie Reynolds and the teachings I've learned at New Light Church. The teachings literally saved my life halfway through this journey.

To Chad Lilly and Prince Camp, Publisher and Editor of InnerCircle Publishing and Revolution Press: Since hosting Prince Camps performance at Mitchie's, you've befriended me during tough times and gave me words of encouragement to continue writing. Your praise of my abilities was sometimes the fuel that got me through very tough days. I thank you both.

To Joyce Hunt, owner of Mitchie's Fine Art and Frame Gallery: You give so much of yourself into the lives of others as you tirelessly and selflessly provide for your son, Mitchie. I can remember well when your only goal was to expose him to the wonder and beauty of his culture through rare art and books that were not being carried by major bookstores and art galleries. Now, this labor of a mother's love has impacted a city, a nation and me. For that, home girl, I thank you.

To Debbie Akers, John Berry, Barbara Carr, Nancy Connelly, Valerie Bridgman Davis, Vicki Goldsberry, Ralph Hausser, Gayle Hight, Ron Horne, Jim Johnson, Byron Kocen, Steve Kocen, Peggy Lynch, Roy Mann and the new members of the Austin International Poetry Festival board: Thank you for the many years of "slugging it out" as a roomful of poets have very passionate opinions and usually just as heated discussions regarding each year's festival. It was an honor and a privilege to record the minutes for the years I was blessed to be on the board. I wish you many years of success. To Talaam Acey, Aqua, Mahogany Browne, Mike Guinn, Nii Parkes, Jive Poetic, Poetical, Shaggy, Queen Sheba and Ebony Washington (POetLITICAL): Thank you for being the traveling poets and prophets that you are. You are the words we need in these latter days. Your encouragement in spoken word has always been in graciousness and love. I thank you.

To Valerie Bridgman Davis (again), Deon Davis, Word Jazz, Kathleen, Ivan Miller, a.k.a. Ivanhoe, Thom the World Poet, Steve Vera (again) and local poets of Austin, Texas: Thank you for keeping me grounded. Austin is not weird: it's honest. It is an honor to perform at your venues and listen to you spit poetry.

To Herman Mason, June Mason and all the poets and producers that have kept Neo Soul Poetry cutting edge in Austin, Texas: Just to hear your words on a Wednesday night is food for the soul. This is a movement that has defied several changes in venue and is a testament to the collective genius that keeps the Soul-diers together.

For that, I thank you all.

References

For some of the quotations in the book,
I used the following web sites:

1. **www.m-w.com**:
Meridian-Webster Dictionary online.

2. **www.quoteland.com**:
for the quotes at the beginning of some chapters.

3. **http://www.poets.org/viewmedia.php/prmMID/15586**:
The Academy of American Poets, specifically the link for the poem by James Weldon Johnson for "Go Down, Death."

4. **www.blueletterbible.org**:
If any quotes are used from the Bible, I farmed them from this site.

Reviews

Reggie:

Once I sat down to read your blog, I could not stop. Here are my thoughts/comments:

I just finished reading the entire blog and it was beautifully written. I've always known you to be an intelligent and extremely talented wordsmith and reading "Unemployed - A Memoir" seals that knowledge. There is a reason you are one of the most talented and respected poets in Austin, Texas. These "spiritual bread crumbs" are needed in today's world. Thank you for sharing.

"I've been on a two-year journey. I've documented the pains I've felt, the self-doubt, the despair, and the hopes. This is a process, long, complicated." You wrote this in the chapter entitled Surrender, and I feel this is the theme that truly underlies your memoir.

From "Great Games of Cat and Mouse" to "Epilogue", I was pulled into a world interlaced with poetry, poignant and pivotal life moments, prolific premonitions and a journey on "Horizon Road" to F.I.N.E (**F**ired up, **I**nspired, **N**aturally talented, and **E**cstatic)

I was especially moved by the account of your father's illness and visiting him in his last days and your undying devotion to him pulled at my heartstrings. "I saw the strong will that kept me from experimenting with the drugs that savaged my community become weak and...frightened." Your dedication to family and the continued support of your wife is wonderful. The Heathcliff Huxtable and Mr. Mom chapters showed a side of the black family that is often overlooked in society.

Your chronicle from the corporate world n to living free and in the confines of talent is real and tragic yet beautiful. I found myself reading certain passages over again and the Biblical references were well placed. The chapter on Faith was eye opening and clearly displays your extraordinary grasps at physics.

I applaud you especially for the mention of the Sun Poet that took her life. It is so true that people suffer in isolation to the point where they feel going on here in this realm is useless. It's a sad testament to not really knowing what a person goes through inside. Depression and suicide is a topic that is not touched on as it should be. So many people suffer in silence and find it hard to escape the glass cage.

All in all, I thank you for including me on this project; wish you the best with InnerCircle (Chad and Prince are wonderful sources of guidance and information)

Be blessed and keep in touch.
Clarissa LeVonne Bolding

In the beginning, the blog seems to be too harsh and reads like a person who is very bitter. The reader can feel the honesty, which draws you to continue through this seemly brutal journal.

Next, the blog moves into a vivid description of a person's dreams and vision for living in America. It's as if the painter's brush touches your eyes to view a masterpiece.

Thanks!
-CC Stinson
CCSquared Productions
P.O. Box 6236
Round Rock, TX 78683
512.740.6860
5127406860@mobile.mycingular.com
www.CCSquared.com

A poet once told me that the most powerful poems often have one of the following two characteristics; the poem either tells a truth few, if any, have ever considered before or the poem tells a truth that everyone knows deep inside themselves but no one dares speak. Many major social reforms of the 50's, 60's, and 70's were the culmination of truths long suffered silently. More and more people, writers, musicians, and preachers, among others, spoke that truth, each turning the wheel of change one degree at a time until the inertia of public dissent kept it rolling perpetually.

Contrary to his reference to Sisyphus, Reggie Goodwin's Unemployed: A Memoir may be the balance of the stone turned one degree beyond the hill's peak. Goodwin does more than put his finger on the pulse of many downsized, Outsourced, unemployed people; he slips it through the skin and into the bloodstream. Besides dealing with the obvious pitfalls of a family man, proud and accomplished, educated, talented and creative being both unemployed and unemployable, he delves into both the expectations imposed by the myth of loyalty between company/industry and employee, as well as the sinister dispense of hope by the droplet that the myth, like unicorns, are real and just around the corner.

Goodwin gives equal portions of raw anger, frustration, and despair, logical and scientific consideration, and personal, spiritual, as well as universal, discovery, enrichment, redemption, and growth. Goodwin's work is a trip on an earthquake-crumpled road only to be repaved by strength found through adversity, with enough left over to build an on-ramp to the scenic route in the lives of others. In Unemployed: A Memoir, Reggie Goodwin erects a signpost to many displaced, disillusioned victims of corporate game theory: hope, joy, and creative living, all pure and plentiful, rest within.

Ron Horne & Dr. Sheila Siobhan, Co-Directors
Texas Youth Word Collective
u21slam@yahoo.com
www.txywc.org
(512)632-5033

Revolution Press

writer to reader...

Catalog of Original Titles

ISBN	Title
0-9755214-4-6	Poem-Made Thoughts by Ron Burroughs
0-9755214-5-4	Shadowboxby Megan Komorowski
0-9755214-0-3	On the Edge of Decency by Rick LaFerla
0-9755214-3-8	Poetry of Hope for Our Times by Colleen Bianchi
0-9762924-9-1	Illumination Without Light by Christopher Aaron
0-9762924-4-0	Simple Poetry A to Z by Janice Sue Andrews
0-9762924-5-9	Panhandle P.I. by M.C. Bechum
0-9762924-6-7	The Journey From Hell by Deborah A. Davis
0-9762924-8-3	The Long Yellow Afternoon by Michael L. Ciavarella
0-9720080-7-1	Quatrains of Our Love by Michael L. Ciavarella

Booksellers!

Are you interested in offering a new genre of books?

Contact us about wholesale offers from

InnerCircle Publishing and **Revolution Press**.

Readers!

Book packages now available!

25% off retail prices!

Visit Us Online!

Follow Your Dream!

www.rev-press.com

INNERCIRCLE PUBLISHING

Catalog of Original Titles

ISBN	Title
0-9720080-9-8	the sometimes girl by Lisa Zaran
0-9720080-2-0	Return To Innocence by Dr. Steven Hairfield
0-9720080-3-9	Interview With An American Monk by Dr. Steven Hairfield
0-9720080-4-7	Interview: Heath and Healing by Dr. Steven Hairfield
0-9723191-4-X	Poetry to Touch the Heart and Soul by Marla Wienandt
0-9755214-9-7	Touched by Spirit by Marla Wienandt
0-9723191-2-3	Because Why? The Journey Once Asked! by Kirstie Silk
0-9723191-9-0	Handwriting on the Wall - ICP Original Anthology
0-9723191-8-2	Stress Fractures by Andew Lewis
0-9723191-6-6	Life Rhymes by Rene Ferrell
0-9723191-7-4	One Hundred Keys to the Kingdom by Prince Camp, Jr.
0-9723191-0-7	the voice by Rick LaFerla
0-9755214-0-3	On the Edge of Deceny by Rick LaFerla
0-9723191-5-8	A Day in the Mind by Chad Lilly
0-9755214-6-2	uncommon sense by Chad Lilly
0-9755214-7-0	Peace Knights of the Soul by Dr. Jon Snodgrass
0-9755214-1-1	Petals of a Flower by Patricia McHenry
0-9755214-2-X	Poetry-Prose-Stories by J.L. Montgomery
0-9762924-0-8	The Weave that Binds Us by Martin Burke
0-9762924-2-4	Dare to Question by Jack Perrine
0-9762974-2-6	The Twelve Mastery Teachings of Christ by Lea Chapin
0-9762924-3-2	Alnombak by Ken Delnero
0-9762924-7-5	Life is a Song Worth Singing by Clarissa LeVonne Bolding
0-9762974-3-4	The Spirit Within by Susan Marie Ratcliffe
0-9720080-8-X	And the Angels Spoke by Rebecca Steiger
0-9762974-5-0	Unemployed - A Memoir by Reginald L. Goodwin

Printed in the United States
64187LVS00003B/163-210

9 780976 297451